Zen

Zen

An ancient path to enlightenment for modern times

PETER OLDMEADOW

LANSDOWNE

Contents

Introduction

Zen is a form of Buddhism with origins in the teachings of the Buddha, who lived and taught in the sixth century BC in what is now northern India and Nepal. Zen developed its most characteristic forms in China. From there, it spread to Korea, Vietnam and Japan. Today, Zen is also firmly established in the West, where new forms of Zen practice and institutions are developing.

FEATURES OF ZEN

Zen shares the basic teachings of the Buddha with other forms of Buddhism, but it gives these its own special emphasis. In addition, it has its own literature, style of teaching and methods of practice.

• Zen Buddhism emphasizes direct realization of the truth and its actualization in the concrete circumstances of our daily life.
• It is based on the Buddha's own experience of Enlightenment, the essence of which it claims to have transmitted through an unbroken series of teachers up until the present day.
• Zen avoids adherence to particular scriptural formulations, dogmatism of any variety, and indulgence in abstract philosophical speculation.
• It offers a practical path embracing a range of skillful methods, and invites us to look into our own minds and hearts where we can find the truth of our own nature.
• Zen stresses meditation as a discipline for formal practice and as a means for living in awareness and appreciation of each moment of our lives.

TYPES OF BUDDHISM

The various types of Buddhism that developed prior to the spread of Buddhism to the West can be broadly classified as belonging either to the Theravada tradition ('tradition of the elders') found predominantly in South-East Asia, or to the Mahayana tradition ('the great way') found in Nepal, Bhutan, Tibet, Mongolia, China, Korea, Japan and Vietnam. Theravada tradition aimed to preserve the original teachings of the Buddha without change. Mahayana Buddhism took a more flexible approach and found expression in a variety of schools and spiritual practices appropriate to different cultural settings.

APPROACHES WITHIN MAHAYANA BUDDHISM ('GREAT WAY' BUDDHISM)

- Cultivation of virtue through actions of body, speech and mind, and avoidance of non-virtue.
- Philosophical Buddhism involving reasoning and analysis.
- Devotional Buddhism based on faith.
- Tantric Buddhism (*Vajrayana*) involving complex meditation practices incorporating aspects of Indian yoga practice and including the repetition of sacred sounds (*mantra*) and elaborate visualizations.
- Approaches that stress simple sitting meditation.

Zen is a form of Mahayana Buddhism that stresses simple sitting meditation. Because of this, it came to be known in China as the Chan School, which means 'Meditation School.' It is better known in the West under the Japanese translation of the name, 'Zen.'

Zen and the Basic Principles of Buddhism

BUDDHA AND HIS ENLIGHTENMENT

The Enlightenment of the Buddha is central to Buddhism. The word 'Buddha' means 'enlightened' or 'awakened.' It refers to a fully enlightened being who has awakened from the sleep of ignorance or who is enlightened about both his or her own nature as well as the nature of the world. Historically, the word 'Buddha' is most often used to refer to Siddhartha Gautama, a prince of the Shakya clan in ancient India (sixth century BC) who, after a long spiritual struggle, had a great spiritual awakening and became the Buddha, the Enlightened One. As the enlightened sage *(muni)* of the Shakya clan, he also came to be known as Shakyamuni Buddha.

In his enlightenment experience, the Buddha gained insight into the suffering or pain that pervades our existence. He discovered a new mode of awareness and way of living driven neither by the grasping of desire nor by the aversion of hatred. This enlightened awareness is free of the ignorance and delusion that is characteristic of our normal consciousness. It finds expression in a host of positive qualities, most importantly, great wisdom and great compassion. These are exemplified in the life of the Buddha.

The Buddha embarked on a long life as a teacher in Northern India in order to communicate this experience, with its liberating knowledge, to others. He founded a community of followers, establishing the basic patterns of institutional life, meditative practice, and philosophical and religious thinking known as Buddhism.

Shakyamuni Buddha, touching the earth to witness to his enlightenment.

8

The teachings of the Buddha are preserved in the Buddhist scriptures *(sutras)*.

SUFFERING IN OUR LIVES

Shakyamuni Buddha said, 'I teach two things: suffering *(duhkha)* and the end of suffering.' These are fundamental to Buddhism as a way of life, as a philosophy and as a religious tradition. The term *duhkha*, usually translated as 'suffering' or 'pain,' refers to the unsatisfactoriness or angst that all people experience. This pain ranges from the obvious agonies of disease and death, to the more subtle feeling of some dissatisfaction or lack of meaning in our lives, despite all the good things that we may have. This subtle kind of pain is illustrated in the life story of the future Buddha.

The young prince Siddhartha Gautama is depicted as having everything one could desire - wealth, bodily beauty, intelligence, a beautiful wife and child, abundant leisure time and so on - yet something was lacking in his life. Despite all that surrounded him, he was still troubled by the fact of death and by the fundamental questions of existence. Awareness of his own and others' pain provided the starting point for Siddhartha's spiritual quest. A long search culminated in Siddhartha becoming the Buddha, the Enlightened One.

SUFFERING AS THE STARTING POINT OF THE PATH

It is said that when the Buddha had his awakening, his great enlightenment experience, he doubted whether he could communicate something so profound to others. After some hesitation, he set out on his quest to teach the knowledge he had gained. Rather than talk about his great experience, even though it is what made him the Enlightened One, Shakyamuni made the fact of suffering and pain the starting point of his teaching. For the Buddha, such an approach is not something to argue about, nor is it a matter of faith. Rather, the acknowledgement of pain is the entry point into a deeper investigation of reality, an opportunity to begin to know things as they are rather than as we might imagine them or wish them to be. The truth of suffering is the first of the Four Noble Truths.

THE FOUR NOBLE TRUTHS:

The truth of suffering, *duhkha*

The truth of the arising of suffering

The truth of the cessation of suffering

The truth of the path to the end of suffering

THE CAUSE OF OUR PAIN

According to the Buddha, the cause of the angst in our lives is to be found in the patterns of clinging and aversion that dominate our minds and govern our actions. From moment to moment, we are driven by the desire to prolong or gain pleasurable experiences and the desire to get rid of or avoid pain. So enmeshed have we become in patterns of desire and avoidance that these patterns have assumed lives of their own and come to control our lives. We do not act in clear awareness, but under the control of often unconscious drives and emotions. Our actions, rather than satisfying our desires, often result in further frustration and antagonism.

OUR ACTIONS - KARMA, CAUSE AND EFFECT

Our ignorant actions are part of a series of cause and effect. They are partly determined by our past actions, which have established habitual patterns or tendencies in our minds. In turn, most of our present actions serve to entrench the patterns of thinking and behaving already established. The Buddha, in line with ancient Indian thought, named action, which is part of a long chain of cause and effect, *karma*. He understood the scope of *karma* to reach beyond our present lifetime through a series of rebirths. In this way, our present life is seen as part of a larger pattern reaching into the past and extending into the future. The ongoing process of birth and death, as accepted by Buddhism and other ancient Indian religions, is termed *samsara*. According to the Buddha, rebirth occurs repeatedly, including within the realms of various other world systems such as heavens, hells, spirit and animal realms.

Interlocking pig, cock and snake representing the interdependence of greed (cock), delusion and ignorance (pig) and hatred (snake).

Unlike some ancient thinkers, the Buddha did not understand *karma* as a kind of fatalism that necessarily controls our lives, determining our destiny no matter what we may do. His understanding was different. The Buddha taught that:

• because most of our actions are done without awareness or understanding of our own motivations and drives, they serve to enmesh us in a series of events we do not understand and cannot seem to control;

• we do not have to act in a way that is predetermined by our past responses - because we have awareness, we can choose how we react;

• the key to breaking the series of unconscious reactions and actions is to bring this awareness into each moment of our lives;

• rather than reacting automatically or unconsciously to our changing circumstances, when we develop awareness we can respond in a way that is free of the habits and the conditioning from our past.

IGNORANCE AND NON-SELF

According to the Buddha, the continuing pattern of clinging and aversion is due to basic ignorance or lack of awareness. Behind our aversion and attachment lies a deep-rooted but essentially mistaken idea of who we are. We mistake ourselves for our fixed idea of ourselves, which is only an abstraction made up from the memories of our life and our past experiences. Our concept of ourselves cannot capture the dynamic reality of our actual existence; it can only give us a frozen picture of a self set apart from the world and other beings. We are so attached to this image (our 'ego') that we take it to be our fundamental identity or our real self. It is this image that we struggle to protect and promote. Under its spell, we hope that we can master our outer circumstances and organize our relationships for its satisfaction.

But, according to the Buddha, we are mistaken about our own identity. We are not who we think we are. The reality of our being is far more than the idea we have of it or, indeed, of any idea that we could have of it. The Buddha taught about *anatman*, or 'non-self,' warning against mistaking or limiting our identity of ourselves with our bodies, feelings and ideas.

THE BUDDHA ANALYZED THE SELF IN TERMS OF FIVE CATEGORIES OR *SKANDHAS*:

- body
- feeling
- perception
- mental formations
- consciousness

He said that none of these five define the self, nor is there some self separate from these. This is the doctrine of 'non-self' *(anatman)*. By meditating on this we break down the belief in the ego.

THE REALITY OF ENLIGHTENMENT

A life based on desire for pleasure and on aversion to pain is not the only way to live. Neither is the answer a kind of stoicism that accepts the inevitability of pain and resolves to endure it. The Buddha claimed to have found in his enlightenment a radical alternative that relieves us of the constant frustration and angst of our lives.

When the Buddha attained enlightenment, he experienced the state of nirvana. Buddhism teaches that nirvana is:

• the end, or 'cooling,' of greed, hatred and delusion;
• the end of suffering;
• the end of the continual round of rebirths fueled by the three poisons of greed, hatred and delusion;
• the end of our wrong idea of self and the clinging and aversion that goes with it. It is not annihilation of self;
• purified awareness. It is not an unconscious state;
• the end of our obsession with our 'self,' not a state of indifference. Enlightenment opens us to others and awakens the great compassion, the great caring, that is the hallmark of an enlightened being.

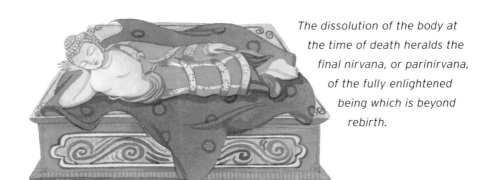

The dissolution of the body at the time of death heralds the final nirvana, or parinirvana, of the fully enlightened being which is beyond rebirth.

THE PATH TO FREEDOM

Buddhism is quintessentially a way or path. In an obvious sense, it is a path that will take us to enlightenment; a path that will take us from pain to the end of pain. However, it is not merely a means to an end. We must not bring our usual acquisitive mind to the Path. Such an approach might suggest that nirvana is a goal that the ego can realize, or an end that we might possess: another project for the satisfaction of the self! Such an approach would be contrary to the Buddhist way, which is aimed at the eradication of grasping, and of the ignorance which lies at the root of it. The true way must reflect the dynamic reality of our own being in each moment rather than our fixed ideas about ourselves.

The Buddha called his way the Noble Eightfold Path. The symbol of the Path is a wheel. Each aspect can be regarded as a spoke in the wheel, and each is essential to the integrity of the whole.

The Wheel symbolizing the Dharma and the Noble Eightfold Path.

The Path can be summarized under three categories, or 'three principal aspects,' that reflect its essential requirements. The three are: conduct, meditation and wisdom. Ethical conduct is the foundation of the Path. It entails non-violence and non-attachment and benevolence towards all other beings. Without ethical conduct, our minds will be too confused to make spiritual progress. Through meditation, we train the mind to be calm so that we are able to see the way things are, and become aware of all our actions and mental states from moment to moment. Wisdom is the actual seeing of the way things are. It allows us to perfect our conduct and our meditation and is the base from which compassion arises.

THE NOBLE EIGHTFOLD PATH

right view	seeing the true nature of things	wisdom *(prajna)*
right intention	not being motivated by desire or aversion being friendly and peaceable being compassionate	
right speech	avoiding lies and false speech avoiding divisive speech avoiding hurtful speech avoiding idle chatter and gossip	conduct *(sila)*
right action	avoiding harming living beings avoiding taking what is not given avoiding sexual misconduct	
right livelihood	not based on harming or exploiting other beings	
right effort	stopping unwholesome states from arising abandoning unwholesome states developing and cultivating wholesome states	meditation *(samadhi)*
right mindfulness	awareness of body awareness of feelings awareness of mental states awareness of thoughts and ideas	
right concentration	developing mental focus	

The Path is also known as The Middle Way. It avoids the extremes of asceticism and indulgence. The Buddha had experienced both, in his life of luxury in the palace and in the early stages of his spiritual search when he renounced his former life and practiced asceticism and bodily mortification. He rejected both extremes, advocating a Middle Way.

Zen and the Great Way of the Mahayana

EARLY DEVELOPMENT OF BUDDHISM

Historical background

In the middle of the first millennium BC, Shakyamuni Buddha taught for some forty-five years along the Ganges plain in Northern India. During his lifetime, he taught people from many different social strata, and established his community comprising ordained monks and nuns, as well as lay men and women. The essential patterns of monastic life were laid down, providing a framework for those who wished to renounce society and dedicate themselves to the Path free of the distractions of worldly life. Evidence suggests that the community grew slowly but steadily in North India in the early years.

The reign of the emperor Ashoka in the third century BC provided a turning point for Buddhism. Ashoka, a convert to Buddhism and its way of non-violence, was instrumental in the promotion of Buddhism and its propagation outside of its original homeland. During his reign, the Buddha's teaching was taken North-West into what is present-day Kashmir and as far South as present-day Sri Lanka. His reign saw the spread of Buddhism throughout the Indian sub-continent with tremendous growth in its numbers and influence.

DEVELOPMENT OF BUDDHIST SCHOOLS

By the third century BC, the break-up of the original Buddhist tradition into a number of sub-traditions had occurred. This partly reflected the spread and diversity of the new community. In this process, two trends were evident: one stressing strict adherence to the original teaching of the Buddha, the other stressing the spirit of the Buddha's teaching rather than literal adherence to the scriptures. The latter tradition argued that the central message of the Buddha was in danger of being lost due to an unwarranted emphasis on the role of the renunciate monk, a remote and austere figure, and because of an excessive emphasis on rules and regulations. This basic division within the community paved the way for the emergence of a new movement within Buddhism that came to call itself the *Mahayana*, the Great Way. Zen Buddhism later grew within this Mahayana tradition as it spread to China, and subsequently to Vietnam, Korea and Japan. The more conservative tradition is today represented by Theravada Buddhism, which is found throughout South-East Asia.

EMERGENCE OF THE MAHAYANA

The Mahayana emerged in the first century BC. According to the Mahayana tradition, more comprehensive teachings had been given by the Buddha to his close disciples during his lifetime than had been publicly taught. It was claimed that these teachings had been withheld until the time was ripe for their dissemination. Accordingly, the Mahayana includes scriptures not found in the earlier collections, and claims that its own teaching gives a clearer account of the Buddha's message. It also claimed that its teachings redress imbalances and distortions that had crept into interpretations of the Buddhist doctrine. Despite argument about the truth of the new scriptures, by the early centuries of the first millennium AD when Buddhism was spreading through Central Asia to China, the majority of the Buddhist community in India had accepted the new teachings as the authentic words of the Buddha. Several features were prominent in the new teachings that had either been absent in the earlier teachings or had been present only in a rudimentary form.

THE PLACE OF THE BODHISATTVA

The Mahayana included a new emphasis on the role of *bodhisattvas*. Bodhisattvas are beings close to becoming fully enlightened who, out of compassion for others, work for their benefit, even to the point of delaying their own final attainment of nirvana. Bodhisattvas were believed to reside in many different world systems, some with conditions far more conducive for spiritual advancement than those found on Earth. The bodhisattvas appealed to the popular imagination, as it was believed that less advanced beings could call on the saving powers of the bodhisattvas to aid them in their spiritual struggles, and even for help in everyday matters.

The bodhisattvas became objects of devotion. Religious movements became associated with popular bodhisattva figures. Prominent among the bodhisattvas was Maitreya, who, it was believed, as the future human Buddha will revive the Buddha's teaching in our world after it has completely disappeared. Some devotees prayed to be reborn in the world system in which he currently resides, or to be reborn in this world at the time Maitreya takes birth to revive the Buddhist teaching here.

The bodhisattva Maitreya.

The bodhisattva Avalokiteshvara was perhaps the most popular, worshipped, as he is today, in many forms. Avalokiteshvara was understood to be the pure expression of compassion, appearing in both male and female guise wherever beings are suffering intensely. In the iconography of his cult, Avalokiteshvara is sometimes represented with a thousand arms, each with a hand available to help struggling beings. In other depictions, Avalokiteshvara is a maternal figure with the love of a mother for her children. In China, Avalokiteshvara became the most popular bodhisattva in the form of Kuan Yin, goddess of compassion.

The bodhisattva of compassion, Avalokiteshvara.

Sometimes bodhisattvas were believed to have become fully realized buddhas, but had only done so on the condition that they could continue to help beings by maintaining a presence in the round of births and deaths (*samsara*). One of these buddhas is Amitabha who, as a bodhisattva, vowed that he would only attain full Buddhahood if he were able to continue to help beings who call his name in faith. According to his devotees, it is only necessary to repeat his name in faith in order to be reborn in his Western Paradise or Pure Land. A devotional form of Buddhism, known as Pure Land Buddhism, became, along with Chinese Zen *(Chan)*, one of the two most popular forms of Buddhism within China and throughout the Far East.

THE INTERRELATEDNESS AND INSUBSTANTIALITY OF ALL THINGS

The earlier Buddhist teaching had taught that all things are impermanent. Because of their impermanence, they provide no basis for lasting satisfaction. Clinging to things while ignorant of their perishable nature can only result in pain. The Mahayana went further. All things, it taught, are not only impermanent, but are ultimately insubstantial and devoid of any individual identity. Negatively stated, this is the doctrine of 'emptiness' or 'no-thingness' (*shunyata*), the doctrine that all things are without independent existence.

It is an extension of the idea of non-self (*anatman*), which had been applied in the earlier teachings to the ego or individual self. In the Mahayana, the idea of non-self is applied more comprehensively to all phenomena. In this way, the teaching of non-self becomes a teaching of no-thingness. That is to say, no individual thing exists by itself. More positively, the teaching points to the interrelatedness of all things. No thing can exist independently on its own, but only in a network of relationships with all other things.

The doctrine of emptiness or no-thingness, properly understood, is not a teaching of nihilism or pure negation, but of interdependence. The wisdom it teaches involves an opening of the heart, which comes with the realization that we are inseparably related to all beings and all things. The unlimited and universal compassion of the bodhisattva is said to flow from this realization. The bodhisattva, with this realization, sees the spiritual destiny of all beings as interrelated, and so can no longer seek his or her own exclusive salvation.

BUDDHA NATURE

The Mahayana, like the earlier teaching, teaches non-self *(anatman)*. According to this teaching, the idea we have of ourselves as permanent separate egos is mistaken. There is no such being. When we cling to this idea, we perform unskillful actions that bind us more tightly to the painful process of change through this life and beyond. Like the teaching of emptiness or no-thingness *(shunyata)*, the teaching of non-self can lead to unbalanced or excessively negative interpretations. Such interpretations could imply our total negation. The Mahayana countered such negativity by stressing that the reality of our being goes far beyond our conception of it. When freed of delusion, we are capable of realizing a profound awareness that expresses itself through an abundance of positive qualities, such as compassion, love, joy, patience and generosity. The potential for this realization is a reflection of our deeper nature, which, in the Mahayana, is termed Buddha nature. Sometimes Buddha nature is envisaged as a seed or potential for enlightenment that we can all cultivate. Just as a seed with the proper cultivation can grow into a mighty tree, so our Buddha potential can grow into the tree of enlightenment. At other times, Buddha nature is seen more radically, not as mere potential but as our fundamental identity, which is always present but may be temporarily obscured. Just as the vastness of the sky is always present, although it may be momentarily covered by clouds, so our fundamental nature is hidden by temporary delusions.

The circle symbolizes emptiness, realization and totality. It is the simplest representation of the experience of shunyata.

Development of Zen in Eastern Cultures

BUDDHISM AND DIFFERENT CULTURES

The teaching of the Buddha is not tied to a particular geographic region nor to a particular culture. From the beginning, Buddhism recognized a clear distinction between the way things fundamentally are and the cultural conventions and arrangements by which people organize their societies and relationships. In this, Buddhism differed from Hinduism, the other great religious tradition born of the soil of India. Hinduism saw its stratification into social classes or castes with their distinct duties and responsibilities as divinely ordained and expressing a cosmic law. Its central revelation was also tied to Indian Motherland with its sacred rivers, mountains and lakes. To be a traditional Hindu is to be rooted in a particular place and within a particular society.

Since Buddhism was not tied to a particular place or culture, it could be transported out of India and could successfully take root in different cultures. Naturally, in order to communicate its message to people of different backgrounds, it accommodated itself to its new environments and found new ways of expressing its fundamental teachings. Thus, Buddhism itself changed while transforming the societies in which it grew. In different parts of Asia, new, and often strikingly contrasting, forms of Buddhism developed.

THE DEVELOPMENT OF CHINESE BUDDHISM

Buddhism arrived in China during the first century AD. It was brought to China by traders and others travelling through Central Asia along the ancient silk routes. Monks bringing Buddhist scriptures followed and by the second century Buddhist texts were being translated into Chinese.

China already had a developed literate culture as well as its own indigenous religious traditions. The Chinese were convinced of their own cultural superiority, so at first there was little sympathy for the new, 'barbarian' tradition. Certain aspects of Indian Buddhism were also alien to the Chinese approach. Indian teaching tended to be highly metaphysical and abstract. The Chinese were practical and oriented to the concrete realities of day-to-day existence. Furthermore, Buddhism had developed in India in an environment of asceticism and renunciation of the world. This was foreign to the Chinese, who valued the family and worldly prosperity.

Only gradually did the emphasis of Buddhism in China change to accommodate Chinese sensibilities. It took several centuries for Buddhism to become firmly established in its new home. The traditions that were successful fell broadly into two categories: those that were essentially a continuation of Indian traditions and those that were distinctively Chinese. Eventually, only those traditions that were distinctively Chinese survived with significant numbers of followers. Chinese Zen (Chan) was one of these traditions.

Yin Yang - Chinese and Taoist symbol representing interrelation and interdependence of opposites

ZEN AND TAOISM

The main religious and philosophical traditions in China at the time when Buddhism arrived were Confucianism and Taoism. Confucianism was primarily concerned with ritual, ethical and legal norms and the establishment of proper human relationships within the framework of Chinese society. Taoism, in contrast, was more interested in the world that lay outside the domain of cultural conventions. It spoke more directly to the spirit, reflecting the spontaneity and creativity of nature and the human imagination, which can never be entirely confined by rules and regulations.

In the early years, some antagonism on the part of Confucians was expressed towards Buddhism. Some Taoists, on the other hand, found Buddhist ideas and meditation appealing, and a fruitful dialogue was established between the traditions. Sympathy was also facilitated by the widespread, but historically implausible, belief that Lao-tzu, the founder of Taoism, had traveled to India at the time of Shakyamuni Buddha, and had perhaps been one of the Buddha's teachers.

Buddhism, like Taoism, taught that reality cannot be captured or adequately expressed through the conventional categories of language, and that the more subtle aspects of reality utterly elude our attempts to grasp them. Both saw themselves as ways or paths towards a realization that is beyond categorization. According to Lao-tzu's famous poem the Tao Te Ching:

The Way that can be named is not the true Way.

The Taoist love of naturalness and spontaneity was particularly influential on the development of Zen. The Tao, the basic principle at the root of all things, works without deliberation and without making a directed effort. According to the Taoists, it acts by *wu-wei*, by non-doing. Likewise, the sage or wise person who lives in harmony with the Tao achieves all that needs to be done without conscious or calculated efforts, almost as if he or she does nothing at all. According to Lao-tzu, 'the Tao does nothing yet everything gets done.' The Tao is both the fundamental principle and the way. To realize the Tao does not require artificiality and conscious control. On the contrary, it is only realized by giving up all artificial contrivances and self-conscious deliberation, allowing spontaneous expression to the inner working of our being. In doing this, the Taoist sage imitates nature, which acts spontaneously and as an organic whole.

THE GREAT CHINESE ZEN TEACHERS

Chinese Zen (Chan) is a form of Buddhism that is in conformity with traditional Chinese thinking, particularly as it found expression in Taoism, but the roots of the tradition lie in India. Zen, like all schools of Buddhism, traces its lineage back to Shakyamuni Buddha. It was brought to China by Bodhidharma, a forceful Indian monk who came to China in the fifth or sixth century AD. He is represented as the twenty-ninth in an unbroken series of Indian teachers or 'patriarchs,' and is reputed to have spent nine years sitting facing a wall. He placed great emphasis on sitting meditation, and because of this, his approach was known by the Indian term for meditation, *dhyana*. This came to be pronounced in Chinese as 'Chan,' and the Chinese School, with Bodhidharma as its founder, was called the 'Chan School.'

The pronunciation became 'Zen' in Japanese, 'Son' in Korean and 'Thien' in Vietnamese.

According to Zen, the origin of the tradition does not lie in doctrines, scriptures, or monastic rules, but in the very enlightenment experience of the Buddha, which was communicated wordlessly to his senior disciple Mahakashyapa in the 'flower sermon.' The Buddha, it is said, once simply held up a flower to the assembled disciples without speaking. Mahakashyapa alone understood the significance of the Buddha's action, had a deep experience of enlightenment and smiled. Shakyamuni said, 'You alone have the true eye of the Dharma,' thus affirming that Mahakashyapa had deeply realized the truth and the essence of the Buddha's teaching.

Bodhidharma meditating facing the wall.

The transmission or communication of this enlightenment experience, which goes beyond words, is at the heart of Zen Buddhism. Scriptures and doctrines are not the key and, consequently, Zen understands itself as a special transmission outside of the scriptures. The act of the Buddha in lifting the flower points directly to the truth without using words. This 'direct pointing' through gesture, deed, shout, or enigmatic saying became a feature of Zen. What is directly pointed to is the true nature of things, in particular our own true nature or Buddha nature.

A VERSE ON THE ESSENCE OF ZEN, ATTRIBUTED TO BODHIDHARMA:

A special transmission outside the scriptures

Not relying on words or letters

Pointing directly to the mind

Seeing into one's nature and becoming a buddha

Bodhidharma, the accepted founder of the tradition in China, marks the beginning of a line of six Chinese 'patriarchs' who gave the tradition a progressively more Chinese form. By the time of the Sixth Patriarch, Hui-neng, Chan had become fully Chinese. So highly regarded was Hui-neng that his teachings were accorded the same status as the Buddhist scriptures (sutras). The story of his life and acceptance as the Sixth patriarch illustrates some important features of Zen.

THE SIXTH PATRIARCH HUI-NENG

Hui-neng is said to have been illiterate, and to have had a deep enlighten-ment experience as a boy when he overheard a snippet of the *Prajna Paramita Sutras* ('Perfection of Wisdom Scriptures') proclaiming the empti-ness and insubstantiality of all things. His alleged lack of learning illustrates that Chan (Zen) does not regard intellectual sophistication as essential to realization of the truth. On the contrary, intellectual thought may even be an impediment. Hui-neng went to live at the monastery of the Fifth Patriarch, who immediately recognized the depth of his realization, but set him to work anonymously in the kitchen for fear that he might suffer the enmity of the senior monks. Later, the Fifth Patriarch announced that he would recognize as his successor the disciple who could best express his understanding of the essence of Buddhism through a poem. It was generally expected that the senior monk, Shen-hsiu, would be recognized as the successor. Shen-hsiu anonymously wrote a poem on the corridor wall of the monastery:

> The body is the Enlightenment tree
> The mind is like a bright mirror standing
> Be careful to continually wipe it
> And not allow dust to settle

Hui-neng, having an even deeper realization, anonymously wrote a poem next to it:

> There never was an Enlightenment tree
> Nor bright mirror standing
> Since all is empty
> Where is dust to settle?

28

The Fifth Patriarch realized that only Hui-neng could have written the second poem, which displays a more radical understanding and deeper penetration. He praised the first poem as being highly beneficial, but secretly conferred the succession on Hui-neng, telling him to remain away from the monastery in the mountains until the inevitable outcry over his succession had subsided. Both Shen-hsui and Hui-neng are said to have established lineages of practice, but only that of Hui-neng has survived.

Both poems reflect aspects of Buddhist understanding, but Hui-neng's expresses a more characteristically Zen viewpoint. The first poem teaches a gradual purification of the mind through meditation practice, whereby the defiling passions and thoughts, the 'dust,' can be eliminated from the mind, resulting in enlightenment. But according to Hui-neng, the mind is not a mirror to which thoughts and passions cling. Rather, both the mind and the thoughts or passions are empty or insubstantial; when this is realized through wisdom or insight, no gradual process of purification is required. The mind reveals its true nature or Buddha Nature, and the thoughts and passions, rather than needing to be eliminated, are transformed, functioning as the natural expression of the positive qualities of enlightenment.

Circle, triangle and square representing all the forms of manifestation.

SUDDEN AND GRADUAL ENLIGHTENMENT

Zen, especially according to the radical understanding of the Sixth Patriarch, believes that enlightenment can occur as a sudden breakthrough or insight. Realization of the truth is not achieved through gradually acquiring a better understanding. Rather, truth must be apprehended as a whole in a completely new way of seeing or experiencing. Our usual way of understanding is through concepts and ideas that allow us to build an image or picture of the world around us. This is useful and necessary for our functioning in everyday life. However, the picture can only ever be an approximation or representation. There is also the danger of mistaking the picture for reality. According to Zen, we continuously make this mistake. The breakthrough of enlightenment experience allows a change from seeing things mediated by our ideas and imagination, to seeing things as they really are. The two ways of seeing are discontinuous, and there must be a radical shift from one to the other.

Many of the stories prevalent in Zen suggest that this breakthrough heralds a change whereby a person suddenly shifts from being an ordinary unenlightened being to a fully enlightened Buddha. A more careful reading reveals that the breakthrough, although affording a true insight into reality, may be no more than a glimpse. Most seekers have a series of breakthroughs or, as these are known in Japanese, *kensho*, in which clarity and insight are deepened. Such kensho, or seeing into one's nature, must be distinguished from great enlightenment *(dai kensho)* in which the final impediments to true seeing are overcome.

Zen master strikes a student to precipitate breakthrough to enlightenment (kensho).

30

The accounts of dramatic enlightenment experiences can also obscure the fact that breakthrough to *kensho* is usually preceded by a long period of spiritual maturation. The breakthrough may be sudden or dramatic, but it rarely occurs without considerable preliminary spiritual searching and meditation on the part of the student. The experience of great masters such as the Sixth Patriarch, who had the experience of great enlightenment after merely hearing a few lines of scripture, must be understood as exceptional.

SAYINGS, DOINGS AND SCRIPTURES

Zen claims to be a special transmission outside the scriptures. The fundamental point here is not a rejection of the scriptures. The great teachers in the tradition have been very familiar with Buddhist sutras and doctrines. Buddhist sutras are also chanted in Zen monasteries. However, the great teachers were aware that attachment to scriptures and doctrines can become an obstacle to clear seeing. They also knew that any teaching or doctrine, no matter how profound, can only be a picture of, or pointer to, the truth.

Zen teachers were particularly conscious of how, in some schools, the pursuit of learning or the study of scripture became an end in itself. For some people, attachment to the rules and forms of monastic life could also substitute for the true life of enlightenment. True enlightenment can never be confined to or captured in holy scriptures, subtle philosophy, or rules and rituals. It must be apprehended directly and lived. The masters were ever ready to expose the self-deception and limitations of their disciples. They demanded of their disciples a direct demonstration of enlightenment expressed in the concrete circumstances of daily life, and they themselves demonstrated their own understanding in the same way. True enlightenment must be evident in the kitchen, the garden, in dealings with friends and strangers, not just in the meditation hall or in learned discourse. Over time, the stories of the actions and the often enigmatic sayings of the masters were collected. These became an important source of inspiration and instruction within Zen. The stories and sayings were especially prized because they did not allow easy intellectual assimilation, but rather teased the mind to seek a more immediate and intuitive understanding. As the number of Zen monks and adherents grew and Zen became more institu-tionalized in China, these sayings and doings were set as topics or problems for meditation in the monasteries. The dialogues and interchanges of the masters are known as *mondo* (Chinese *wen-ta*), and the cases or problems they present are known as *koans* (Chinese *kung-an*). Koans are not nonsen-sical or meaningless as is sometimes stated, but they do defy complete understanding at the level of the rational or conceptual mind. Here is an example of such a dialogue:

Question: Where are you going?
Answer: To an unchanging place.
Question: If it is unchanging, how can there be any going?
Answer: Going too is unchanging.

FURTHER DEVELOPMENT OF CHINESE ZEN

The Chinese Zen transmission is said to have passed through five patriarchs, beginning with Bodhidharma. The transmission to the Sixth Patriarch was disputed. The dispute hinged on whether the title of patriarch had passed to the senior disciple of the Fifth Patriarch Shen-hsiu or to the young and untutored Hui-neng. This dispute reflected a split between the Southern School stemming from the teachings of Hui-neng and the the Northern School following the teaching of Shen-hsiu. Eventually, the Southern School won the dispute, with Hui-neng accepted as the true Sixth Patriarch and effective second founder of Chinese Zen.

Despite the ascendence of the Southern School and the eclipse of the Northern School, the different emphases of the two schools reflected two approaches to practice that have remained in Zen up to the present day. Hui-neng emphasized sudden enlightenment and the dramatic breakthrough of kensho while Shen-hsui emphasized constancy in practice and gradual purification of the mind resulting finally in enlightenment.

For a period, five schools of Chinese Zen flourished but by the end of the ninth century only two remained. These were the Lin-chi (Japanese *Rinzai*) School and the Tsao-tung (Japanese *Soto*) School. The former stressed sudden enlightenment and meditation on the koan; the latter stressed simple sitting practice and the gradual maturation of the student. The Lin-chi (Rinzai) School drew its inspiration from Hui-neng and a series of brilliant and often unconventional teachers in Tang dynasty China, including Lin-chi (died 867 AD), the founder of the School. Tsao-tung (Soto) looked back to Bodhidharma and his emphasis on sitting meditation. It did not see kensho as the main goal of practice.

Lin-chi, founder of the Lin-chi (Rinzai) school of Zen Buddhism.

33

Later developments saw Chinese Zen incorporate aspects of Pure Land Buddhism, including invocation of the name of the Buddha of the Western Paradise, Amitabha (Chinese *Amitofo*, Japanese *Amida*). This syncretic form of Zen is sometimes referred to as Ming Zen because it was in the Ming dynasty (1368-1644 AD) that it developed.

KOREAN ZEN - SON

Amitabha, Buddha of the Western Paradise.

Buddhism was transmitted to Korea directly from China. It played a major role in the formation of the Korean state. Koreans traveled to China and studied under Zen masters there. They founded monasteries in the remote mountains of Korea and were referred to as the Nine Mountains Schools. Korean Zen, known as Son, became a major force after the ninth century. Its most influential figure was Chinul (1158-1210 AD) who established a purely Korean form. He stressed the usefulness of study of the scripture while attempting to harmonize gradual and sudden approaches to enlightenment. He saw sudden awakening and gradual cultivation as like two wheels of a cart: both are necessary. The use of koans remained important in Korean Zen, although the complex system of koans characteristic of later Japanese Buddhism was never adopted.

VIETNAMESE ZEN - THIEN

Vietnam was influenced by Mahayana forms of Buddhism from China as well as the Theravada Buddhism predominant throughout most of South-East Asia. In the North, devotional Pure Land Buddhism became popular among the ordinary people while Zen (Vietnamese *Thien*) was practiced in the monasteries. In the South, a mixture of Mahayana, Theravada and Hinduism was found. Vietnamese Zen, throughout history, has reflected the influence of Theravada Buddhism with its stress on simplicity, monastic discipline and the practice of continual mindfulness as the surest path to enlightenment.

DEVELOPMENT OF ZEN IN JAPAN

Buddhism was officially introduced to Japan in 538 AD from Korea as part of a diplomatic mission. Later that century, Buddhism was made the state religion of Japan, and the various schools of Chinese Buddhism were introduced along with many aspects of Chinese culture.

RINZAI TRADITION

Zen was not established as a separate school until the monk Esai (1141–1215 AD), introduced the Chinese Lin-chi (Japanese *Rinzai*) form of Zen. Esai also brought tea from China, which he planted in the monastery gardens. Tea-making and drinking as a Zen art developed from this time.

The discipline of Zen with its indifference to death appealed to the samurai warrior class, and a close relationship between Rinzai Zen and the samurai was forged. Esai's students ensured that Rinzai took firm root in Japan. Under imperial patronage, many Chinese masters visited Japan. The koan system was firmly entrenched as central to Rinzai practice.

The most influential master in the Japanese Rinzai tradition was Hakuin (1685–1768). He spent years of wandering and studying with teachers of both the Rinzai and Soto traditions. He was a prolific writer and painter. He reorganized the koan system and revitalized Rinzai Zen by making it available to the common people. In his 'Song of Zazen' he wrote:

> Sentient beings are primarily buddhas:
> It is like ice and water,
> Apart from water ice cannot exist;
> Outside sentient beings where do we find buddhas?
> Not knowing how near the Truth is
> We seek it far away – what a pity!
> We are like him who in the midst of water,
> Cries out in thirst so imploringly.

35

SOTO TRADITION

The Soto tradition in Japan was founded by Dogen (1200-53). He studied Rinzai Zen in Japan before travelling to China. Dogen's understanding of Zen stems from his insight into the spiritual problem that had gripped him. Why, he asked, given that we all possess Buddha nature as affirmed in the sutras, do we need to engage in strenuous spiritual practice? Why, if the unsatisfactory world is not other than the ultimate, do we need to strive to realize nirvana? Dogen resolved this question and experienced deep enlightenment after he met a monastery cook in China who opened his eyes to Zen. Dogen realized that Buddha nature is not something that we possess in the sense of having or owning. For Dogen, Buddha nature must be realized from moment to moment, and the activity that realizes it is called 'practice.' In Dogen's Zen, practice and realization are inseparable. Practice has no end, nor does it arrive anywhere. Practice is the manifestation of ultimate reality. The Soto School emphasizes 'just sitting' or *shikantaza*. In this practice, there is no seeking, no hope of gain, and no striving for enlightenment. Enlightenment is to be found in the simple act of sitting, or cooking, or washing dishes or any other activity. Dogen wrote:

> The life of one day is a life to rejoice in. Because of this if you live for just one day, if you can be awakened to the truth, that one day is vastly superior to an eternal life.

The kitchen and cooking has always been important in Zen. Monastery cooks figure in many Zen stories.

36

OBAKU SCHOOL

A third but smaller school of Zen in Japan is the Obaku School. It was introduced from China in the seventeenth century when contact with Chinese Zen was re-established after a long break. The Zen of Ming dynasty China included elements from other Buddhist Schools. Obaku Zen uses koans, but also includes invocation of the name of Buddha Amitabha, who is known as 'Amida' in Japanese. According to Obaku Zen, Amida does not reside outside the mind, but is the Buddha present within all beings. Tetsugan (1630-1682), an outstanding Japanese monk of the Obaku tradition, initiated an edition of the Buddhist scriptures that included writings of all the Buddhist sects.

JAPANESE ZEN TEACHERS AND THE WEST

Zen in Japan, like religious traditions everywhere, has struggled against institutionalization and corruption. Many of the Zen teachers who were instrumental in bringing Zen to the West believed that Japanese Zen was losing this struggle, succumbing to excessive formality and debasing the dharma transmission through hereditary privilege and bribery. They thought that the monasteries were characterized by laxity in practice and realization. They were interested in revitalizing Zen practice in Japan in what they regarded as a time of degeneration. They also hoped that in a new environment, Zen might take root and display renewed life. It was with this motivation that they brought Zen to the West.

Japanese Zen temple

Zen Practice

WHAT IS ZEN PRACTICE?

The Buddha's Fourth Noble Truth describes the Path to the end of suffering. Zen practice is a method by which we move along the Path from suffering to release from suffering. Practice is not confined to what we do on the meditation cushion. It encompasses our behavior and lifestyle, the development of concentration and good qualities of mind in meditation and daily life, and the perfection of our understanding or wisdom. These correspond to the three principal aspects of the Noble Eightfold Path: conduct, meditation and wisdom.

Zen practice is not understood only as a means to an end. It is also the expression of enlightened living. In this sense, practice is not about arriving at a particular place or spiritual goal but about expressing our true nature, our Buddha nature, from moment to moment in our lives. Zen is part of the Mahayana tradition and emphasizes the bodhisattva ideal. According to Zen, the bodhisattva embodies or best expresses enlightened activity in the world. Bodhisattvas are not worshipped in Zen as they are in some schools, but they do provide the model that Zen practitioners hope to emulate. Bodhisattvas are not necessarily supernormal or celestial beings. Anyone who acts for the benefit of others could be a bodhisattva.

THE ASPIRATION TO LIVE THE LIFE OF A BODHISATTVA IS EXPRESSED IN THE VOW:

Though sentient beings are numberless, I vow to save them

Though greed, hatred and delusion arise endlessly, I vow to cut them off

Though the dharma is immeasurable, I vow to understand it

Though Buddha's way is beyond attainment, I vow to embody it fully.

The Zen practitioner knows that he or she may never be able to fulfil these vows but aspires to do so. In this sense also, practice is endless. The main point is not arriving somewhere, but rather the path by which we go and the aspiration by which we live.

AIMS OF MEDITATION PRACTICE

People undertake Zen practice for a variety of reasons. Sometimes the reasons have very little to do with Buddhism or enlightenment. The practice of meditation is very beneficial for bodily health and for a general sense of well-being. Just as the postures or breathing exercises of Indian Hatha Yoga can be practiced for their beneficial effect on the mind and body, so Zen practice can be undertaken without reference to religion or philosophy for its life-enhancing effects. In fact, practice undertaken with the simple motivation of leading a healthier life can have the benefit of being free of spiritual grasping, so it may lead naturally to a deeper search and a deeper realization.

Some people undertake practice in order to calm and focus the mind. Zen practice leads to an enhanced capacity to concentrate and to remain focused on the task at hand. People who lead busy and demanding lives often feel that the cultivation of concentration diminishes the fragmentation and agitation they feel in their daily life, allowing them to operate more efficiently and calmly in undertaking their tasks. Time set apart each day for meditation practice can provide a sanctuary from the 'busy-ness' of life, as well as an opportunity to restore mental clarity and emotional vitality.

Some people practice meditation in order to attain extraordinary powers. The literature in many different spiritual traditions attests that control of the mind can bring about such results. The ability to withstand extreme heat and cold, the ability to do without anaesthesia for surgical procedures, and the experience of clairvoyance are some commonly mentioned examples. Spiritual traditions warn that these and similar powers can pose risks to those aiming to follow a spiritual path. There is the risk that these powers could be pursued as an end in themselves and thus divert the meditator from the central task. This task is understood in Buddhism as diminishing greed, hatred and delusion and cultivating the positive qualities of Buddhahood. A further risk is that the meditator might mistake such side-effects of concentration as signs of spiritual attainment.

True spiritual practice, according to Zen, involves an appreciation that the problem of suffering is not amenable to a permanent solution through purely worldly means. Our pain or angst will not be decisively overcome by merely satisfying our material needs nor by the satisfaction of our appetites. A more fundamental need exists that cannot be satisfied by any amount of sensory indulgence nor through any kind of worldly success or the acclamation of others. Practice also requires an acknowledgement that our actions have consequences for us and others, along with a willingness to accept responsibility for them. In Buddhism, this is understood in the context of karma, the moral law of cause and effect.

Zen practitioners in sitting meditation (zazen).

The aspiration to go beyond suffering is recognized as fundamental to Buddhism. All Buddhists agree that a person can realize nirvana and the end of rebirth. Zen, as part of Mahayana tradition, sees this aim as potentially one-sided and possibly self-centered. Zen believes that this formulation needs a positive side in order to avoid a potential imbalance. Accordingly, Zen sees the final aim of practice in terms of overcoming the negative aspects of our lives and actualizing the positive qualities of buddhas and bodhisattvas. Buddhas and bodhisattvas transform emotional and intellectual poisons, awaken to their own (and others') Buddha nature, and realize the Way in daily life.

FUNDAMENTALS OF MEDITATION PRACTICE

Every activity in life can be part of Zen practice: sitting, lying down, walking, eating, interacting with others. No matter what we are doing, each moment offers us the opportunity to practice mindfulness and awareness, and to cultivate positive qualities such as patience, generosity and love. In higher practice, means and ends coalesce. Practice becomes the expression of our Buddha nature. Our daily activities can express Buddha nature just as can sitting on a meditation cushion or chanting scriptures.

All activities provide fruitful opportunities for practice, but with the pace of modern life, for most of us, awareness is fragmentary and our minds disturbed. We need some special period set aside when we can calm the mind and cultivate concentration. Without this, any kind of practice is very difficult. With meditation practice, the waves of thoughts in the mind settle and the mind becomes like still water. This calmness carries over into our daily activities, allowing us to begin integrating our practice and our daily life.

There is nothing equal to wearing clothes and eating food.
Outside this there are neither Buddhas nor Patriarchs.

Zenrin Kushu

TIME AND PLACE

Most Zen teachers recommend that it is best to set aside a regular time for sitting meditation *(zazen)* each day. This should be a time when you will not be disturbed. In the early morning, the mind is more alert, and there is less chance of being interrupted. The benefits of meditation done in the morning carry into the day's activities. Other meditators prefer the evening. Meditation in the evening helps restore mental equilibrium after the day's activities and ensures a good sleep. Some people like to sit both morning and evening.

It is best to begin with short periods of meditation. Many teachers recommend beginning with sessions as short as ten or fifteen minutes, increasing them gradually to about twenty-five minutes. The quality of practice is more important than the length of time you sit. Establishing a regular pattern and not missing sessions is important. Regular short meditation sessions are much more beneficial than irregular longer ones.

Setting aside a fixed place for meditation is a good idea. A separate room is ideal, but any clean fresh space dedicated to meditation is fine. Many people like to have a low table with flowers, incense and an image of an inspiring figure such as Shakyamuni Buddha, a great bodhisattva or an inspiring teacher. Others prefer a spare uncluttered environment free of images and paraphernalia.

One can sit alone or with others. To sit alone cultivates self-reliance and confidence. To sit with others provides support and helps promote the bodhisattva spirit. Many cities and towns in the West now have Zen groups who meet regularly for meditation. Even two people sitting together can constitute a group. Groups also sometimes organize intensive meditation retreats or *sesshin* where students can set aside a few days or a week to devote themselves to collective Zen practice.

Half lotus posture

POSTURE

The critical factor in posture is a straight back. Ideally, the spine should curve slightly inwards at the lower back, and the belly should be relaxed and not restrained in any way. Ears and shoulders should be in line; the chin pulled in. The center of gravity of the body should be in the lower abdomen, slightly below the navel in the area known in Japanese as the *hara*. This eases tension that accumulates in hunched shoulders, strained neck and constricted stomach. With attention resting in the *hara*, energy flows freely through the body, breathing becomes easy and the mind settled. Hands should rest in the lap, the left hand on top of the right, fingers aligned at the middle joints, and the thumbs lightly touching each other. Taken as a whole, this position gives a sense of bodily and mental integration.

Most Zen teachers recommend that the eyes should remain partially open and the gaze be lowered without being focused on anything in particular. The mouth should be closed with the tongue lightly touching the back of the upper teeth. Although these are the common recommendations of Zen teachers, in actual practice there are many minor individual variations. These variations should not be a matter for concern. Mental alertness and bodily ease are the primary requirements; the various recommendations concerning posture aim to facilitate that.

Zazen using a low bench stool.

POSITION OF LEGS AND SEATING

The position of the legs is partly determined by physical flexibility. The ideal is the full lotus posture with left foot on the right thigh and right foot on the left. This is difficult or impossible for most people. The half-lotus posture with the left foot on the right thigh and the right foot tucked under provides an alternative. Another alternative is the Burmese position with one leg in front of the other resting on the floor or meditation mat. Comfortable posture in these positions is facilitated by using a meditation cushion or *zafu* which raises the buttocks off the ground and allows the knees to be comfortably grounded. The appropriate height for the cushion varies from individual to individual. Kapok filled cushions provide adequate firmness and can be adjusted to fit individual requirements. Knees can be cushioned from the ground by using a meditation mat. Stores that sell books on meditation sometimes also sell meditation cushions and mats.

If one of these positions is not possible, sitting comfortably on a low bench stool or a firm chair, with spine straight, hands on the lap and feet on the floor, is also satisfactory.

Zazen posture using a chair.

BREATHING

Traditionally, Buddhist meditation is divided into calming meditation, which results in mental tranquility or concentration, and insight meditation, which results in wisdom. This division does not feature prominently in Zen and is, in fact, rejected as applying to true Zen practice. Nonetheless, in the early stages of practice, most teachers stress the need to cultivate mental calm and concentration. The usual way of doing this is through meditation on the breath.

Although a range of objects may be used to serve as a focus for concentration, the breath is regarded as ideal. Meditation on the breath is practiced in most Buddhist traditions. The breath is with us as long as we live, thus is always available. Because the patterns of our breathing are connected to both our bodily and mental states, attention to the breath helps us become more aware of both our body and our mind. The breathing process is experienced through immediate bodily sensations that help to anchor us in the present moment rather than in thoughts about the past or the future. As our body and mind become calm, the breath becomes more subtle, while the attention that follows it becomes more refined.

COUNTING THE BREATH

Concentration may be developed through counting the breath, numbering each breath from one to ten, then beginning again. Inhalations or exhalations may be numbered. Many people count both inhalations and exhalations. When the mind wanders, as it inevitably and continually will, attention should be gently returned to the breath and the counting process. Mental wandering should not be regarded as a failure, nor should success be measured in terms of ability to stay with the counting process. One should gently let go of ideas of success and failure, and simply pay attention to the immediate task. Although counting the breath may be regarded as a preliminary method on the Zen path, it does require our full attention and engagement. We will quickly realize how easily distracted we are and how long a time can pass before we realize that our mind has wandered.

The aim of the practice is not to eliminate or suppress thoughts, but to learn to focus and not be led astray by the thoughts that continually arise. Concentration practice is not a kind of fixation, nor exclusion of thoughts. It is a process of relaxing and letting go. If the thoughts are not followed, they subside by themselves. Counting the breath is an aid or skillful method to help us do this.

FOLLOWING THE BREATH

Another practice involves using the breath as a support for meditation without counting inhalations or exhalations. This helps to develop concentration in the same way that counting the breath does. It also serves as an entry into deeper Zen practice. In this practice, we follow our breathing. We are aware of the movement of the breath in each inhalation and exhalation and become fully one with it. We don't think, 'I breathe.' That would be adding something extra. There is no judgement and no attempt at achievement. For us at that moment, the movement of the breath is all there is. As our mind becomes calm and pure, the flow of breath becomes a universal expression of our fundamental nature, our Buddha nature. The breath becomes a fundamental activity of our own being and of the entire universe.

SHIKANTAZA – 'JUST SITTING'

Meditation on the breath can lead seamlessly into what many Zen practitioners consider the highest form of meditation, *shikantaza* or 'just sitting.' Shikantaza is meditation beyond purpose. Shikantaza is sitting as an expression of Buddha nature. It does not involve a struggle for the breakthrough of *kensho* or the enlightenment experience of *satori*. This type of practice was exemplified by Dogen Zenji, the thirteenth century master who brought the Soto School to Japan. The Soto School favors this method, whereas the Rinzai school places more stress on koan meditation and the sudden breakthrough to enlightenment. Practitioners of shikantaza understand enlightenment to be present from the very beginning and zazen to be its fundamental expression. According to Dogen, 'The zazen of even beginners manifests the whole of their essential nature.' In shikantaza, all striving is abandoned, body and mind are 'dropped.' There is no method or special technique in shikantaza; even the effort to follow the breath is abandoned. Nothing needs to be added and there is nothing to be gained. Practice and enlightenment are understood as one. Enlightenment experiences may come in shikantaza but they are not the main point.

Although shikantaza is supremely simple, its very simplicity makes it difficult for beginners. Beginners usually need a skillful method, such as meditation on the breath or work on a koan, as a prop for their efforts and a focus for the mind. The practice of shikantaza by the beginner, in the absence of such aids, can easily degenerate into mere passivity. Critics of the widespread use of shikantaza point out that even Dogen practiced koan meditation for many years before devoting himself to shikantaza.

KOANS

One of the unique features of Zen is the use of koans as a principal method of practice. Koans originated in the sayings and doings of the masters. These were collected and constitute an important part of Zen tradition. Over time, their use as objects for meditation became a formal part of Zen practice. Many of these sayings and interchanges are puzzling and enigmatic. They may involve a dialogue between master and student, an enigmatic question, a shout, a gesture or even silence. The 'flower sermon' in which Shakyamuni Buddha held up a flower without speaking and Mahakashyapa experienced enlightenment is such an interchange. On other occasions, the Buddha is said to have responded with a 'noble silence' when questioned on certain matters. He was not refusing to answer. His silence pointed to a deeper answer, and invited direct understanding or insight on the part of the questioner. Koan practice involves meditation on these sayings and doings with an attempt to fathom and directly experience their significance.

Usually a koan presents a problem or barrier to the rational mind. This does not mean that the koan is meaningless. The student must find the meaning at a deeper level than normal thinking that operates with fixed categories and mutually exclusive alternatives such as 'yes' and 'no.' The student must break through the confines of a mind bound to ego-consciousness and realize a more comprehensive vision. Some well-known koans include, 'What is the sound of one hand?' and 'What was your original face before your parents were born?'

A Zen master holds up one hand and asks his disciple 'What is the sound of one hand?'

50

Usually, a koan is assigned to a student by a teacher or Zen master *(roshi)*. The student is instructed to meditate on the koan, demonstrating to the master his or her understanding of the action, dialogue or question it contains. The teacher will not be satisfied by an intellectual answer that might merely mean the student has only thought about the koan or has an *idea* of its significance. The student must realize the meaning of the koan directly. The student must *know* the answer in his or her very bones. No single correct answer exists to a koan. Looking up the answer in a book or getting someone to tell you would be pointless. The 'answer' must be discovered by the students themselves.

THE KOAN 'MU'

The most widely used koan today comes from an exchange between the great Chinese master Joshu (Chinese, Chao-chu) and a monk. This exchange is recorded in a thirteenth century collection called the *Mumonkan* ('The Gateless Gate'). The monk asked, 'Does a dog have Buddha nature or not?' Joshu replied, 'Mu.' Literally this answer means 'No.'

This would seem to be in flat contradiction to the Mahayana Buddhist teaching, well known to the monk, that all beings have Buddha nature. The questioner is perhaps doubting his own Buddha nature and inquiring whether even a dog could be a Buddha. The reply of the master cuts all this speculation asunder. With its apparent contradiction of the Buddhist scriptures, the master's retort poses a problem for the student. Clearly the significance of this 'mu' cannot be a simple negation. But what then is it? Joshu's mu is pointing directly at the truth of Buddha nature, not the idea of it, nor to questions about it. Joshu invites and challenges the questioner to experience the truth of Buddha nature for himself.

The koan 'mu' is regarded as a particularly effective koan because it allows no place for the intellect to get a hold. It cuts off the 'mind road.' The student knows that there is an answer, that mu is significant. A 'great doubt' arises as to what that answer might be. According to the compiler of the collection in which this koan is found, the student must pour himself or herself into this koan with all '360 bones in the body and all the 84,000 hair follicles.' 'Gradually you purify yourself, eliminating mistaken knowledge and attitudes you have held from the past. Outside and inside become one, and you are like a dumb person who has a dream. You know it for yourself alone. Suddenly mu breaks open. The heavens are astonished; the earth is shaken ... A single spark lights your dharma candle.' This is *kensho* or *satori*, the sudden breakthrough to enlightenment.

REQUIREMENTS FOR SUCCESSFUL PRACTICE

Traditionally, it is said that for any practice, but especially koan practice, to be effective, there are three requirements. These are faith, doubt and determination.

Faith in Zen means the strong conviction that enlightenment is real and that it can be realized. Without this conviction, one will not begin on the path to enlightenment or will abandon it at the first sign of obstacles.

The second requirement is doubt. Faith by itself is not enough. There must be some questioning or some problem that engages the mind. This may arise in us naturally with questions such as, 'Why is there suffering in the world?,' 'Who am I?' or 'Why does Buddhism teach that we are intrinsically perfect and have Buddha nature when our actions and experiences seem to suggest the opposite?' These sorts of questions can arise as 'natural koans' that motivate us along a spiritual path. Alternatively, a koan can engender this kind of doubt in us. At first, the doubt may be somewhat artificial, but if we engage fully in the koan, the doubt becomes very much alive. The question can take on life or death significance. Zen literature is full of stories of seekers being pushed to the extremity of despair by their need to resolve the doubt that has gripped them.

The third requirement is determination. This grows out of the other two requirements and involves the commitment to resolve the doubt, never abandoning the path no matter what obstacles may arise.

Koan practice is difficult without a highly qualified teacher, and is not suitable for all people. The teacher must set a suitable koan for the student and be able to test and recognize the student's understanding. The teacher must be able to guide the student through the difficulties of koan practice, particularly through the despair that he or she may feel at being unable to 'solve' the koan. The teacher must encourage the student, ensuring that he or she does not abandon the search or succumb to spiritual anguish. For most people, koan practice is not recommended in the absence of this guidance.

MEDITATION RETREAT

Effective koan practice usually requires either a monastic setting or periods of intense meditation retreat called *sesshin*. Without this, it is difficult to build up the intensity of concentration required for the breakthrough to *kensho*. The intensity of practice is heightened by long hours of practice, silence, inspirational talks or *teisho* from the teacher, frequent meetings with the teacher called *dokusan*, and by the collective energy of many meditators involved together in a common task. Sesshin are traditionally of seven days duration, although longer and shorter periods are also common. The only talking is with the teacher at formal meetings during which difficulties encountered in practice are discussed or the understanding of the student is tested. Meals are communal and usually eaten in the meditation hall or *zendo*. A period is devoted to chanting the scriptures each day. Sesshin involves energetic all-day sitting. Typically, during sesshin, the day's meditation begins around 4 a.m. and continues through until 9 or 10 at night.

WALKING MEDITATION – KINHIN

Periods of sitting meditation are punctuated by walking meditation or *kinhin*. Kinhin serves to relieve the stiffness in the legs and refresh the mind, but it is not a break from meditation. If the meditators are working on a koan, they will continue to do so while walking. Otherwise, kinhin is a kind of meditation in motion with meditators walking with full awareness of the movement of the legs and body and the inhalation and exhalation of the breath. Styles of walking vary: some walk briskly and energetically, others slowly with deliberate attention to each movement. Twenty-five-minute sitting meditation periods are usually interspersed with five-minute kinhin.

WORK PRACTICE – SAMU

Retreats include periods of manual work or *samu* such as cleaning rooms, sweeping the paths, washing dishes or gardening. This is based on a tradition of self-reliance among Zen communities. According to an old Chinese Zen maxim, 'A day of no work is a day of no eating.' But more is involved than this. Work practice involves giving oneself to the task at hand with undivided attention. It requires a full but mindful engagement in whatever task one is doing. This is not a break from meditation or an impediment or interruption to meditation. Work carried out with full awareness is meditation itself. To actualize the Way in daily life is at the heart of the Zen path. Zen abounds with stories of meditators having deep enlightenment experiences while involved in such simple tasks as sweeping the path or fetching water.

Zen and the Arts

One way to approach Zen is through the arts. Many kinds of Zen art are practiced, including painting and calligraphy, poetry, the tea ceremony, flower arranging, martial arts, archery and gardening. Mastery of a Zen art is not simply the acquisition of a skill; it involves entry into the Way and personal transformation. The artist must become one with his or her work or activity, learning to act spontaneously and without premeditation, yet in harmony with the materials and circumstances. Since Zen involves actualizing the Way, almost any regular activity can become a means of learning about the Way, living in accordance with it and expressing it in daily life. In Japan, where the culture was profoundly influenced by Zen, almost every art or profession can be regarded as a Way (*Do*, Chinese *Tao*).

PAINTING AND CALLIGRAPHY – SUMI-E

Zen painting is not regarded principally as representing nature. Nor is it symbolic like much religious art in Buddhism and other religions. Painting and calligraphy are regarded, like nature, as an expression of the Tao itself. Painting done with black ink on paper or silk, often combined with a poem, became the most common form. Landscapes and figures from Buddhist history or legend are the most common subjects. Just as the Tao acts through non-acting *(wu-wei)*, so the production of art should be uncontrived and spontaneous. Paradoxically, learning to act spontaneously involves discipline and a long training. For example, under the critical gaze of the teacher, a student may practice writing a single Chinese character for days or even weeks until he or she can paint immediately without hesitation or deliberation. The work itself must express the Tao. Often this is achieved as much by what is not represented (the 'emptiness' of the painting) as by the forms depicted.

56

TEA CEREMONY - CHA-NO-YU

In China, tea was used by monks as a mild stimulant for their meditation and was drunk unhurriedly and mindfully. The drinking of tea became associated in Japan with a formalized ceremony. Sen-no-Rikyu (1521-1591), the most famous exponent of the art, defined the requirements for the tea ceremony as harmony, tranquility, purity and respect. Ideally, the tea ceremony is shared by a small number of people (at most five) in a separate small tea house set amid tranquil gardens. The tea ceremony can be seen as a kind of meditation in action that involves the mindful approach to the tea house, sitting with awareness on straw mats, enjoying the aesthetics of the hanging scrolls and utensils used in the ceremony, the preparation of the tea by the host, and the mindful drinking of tea.

Entering into the spirit of the tea ceremony does not require all the ingredients and formality of the traditional Japanese tea ceremony. All that is required are bowls, tea and hot water, and an appreciation of the unhurried, relaxed and simple atmosphere, either alone or with friends. The Vietnamese Zen master Thich Nhat Hahn suggests the following verse when taking a cup of tea:

This cup of tea in my two hands -
mindfulness is held uprightly!
My mind and body dwell
in the very here and now.

*Preparation of tea in
the tea ceremony.*

ZEN AND MARTIAL ARTS

Zen is associated with the martial arts in both China and Japan. In Japan, the acceptance of Rinzai Zen as a Buddhist School was tied to its acceptance and patronage by the samurai warrior class. The samurai ethic harmonized with discipline, spartan spirit, spontaneity and fearlessness in the face of death, which Zen promoted. Rarely did a samurai have any important material wealth apart from his sword. Swordsmanship came to be regarded as an expression of the way of Zen. Sword-making became an art as respected as painting. The samurai lived a life of frugality and discipline and was willing to give his life in defense of his master and honor. The training of samurai became associated with Zen temples; samurai were required to train with koans. They were trained to center themselves in the *hara*, a spot in the abdomen just below the navel, and to use the breath to focus the mind. The warrior trained himself to be empty of ego, to act without premeditation and without ideas of winning or losing, life or death. He trained himself to enter a state of 'no mind' from which he could act with amazing precision and without conscious intent. Similar principles apply to other martial arts and to archery.

ZEN POETRY - HAIKU

Haiku is the poetic expression of Zen moments or Zen consciousness of moments of perception. The poems use seventeen Japanese syllables to directly point to the 'isness' or 'suchness' of things just as they are in the present moment. In Buddhism, all things are regarded as insubstantial, yet as momentarily present in their unique 'suchness.' Haiku, like all Buddhist arts, expresses the idea of the inseparability of 'emptiness' and 'form.' The essence of the art is to capture both simultaneously through what is not expressed (the 'emptiness') and what is expressed (the 'form'): in poetry, silence and sound; in painting, the white paper or silk and the ink or paint. In the work of art, the writer's ego must not intrude. The development of haiku was largely the work of Basho (1643-94), the most famous exponent of the art.

The stars on the pond;
Again the winter shower
Ruffles the water

This road!
With no one going -
Autumn evening

In the utter silence
Of a temple
A cicada's voice alone
Penetrates the rocks

Western Zen

SOURCES OF WESTERN BUDDHISM

Before the colonial period in the eighteenth and nineteenth centuries when much of Asia came under European control, Western knowledge of Buddhism and other Asian religions was fragmentary. In the colonial period, a rudimentary knowledge of Asian religions was gained as scholars began to study and make available the classical religious texts of India and China. Some Europeans and Americans who read these texts were drawn to Asian religions because they believed they offered an alternative to the growing rationalism and materialism of Europe and America. Others thought that Hinduism, Buddhism and Taoism might be an attractive alternative to the Judaism and Christianity with which they were familiar.

The Theosophical Society, which was founded in the United States in 1875, did much to promote popular interest in Buddhism. The movement was established to foster the study of Western esoteric traditions such as Hermeticism and Alchemy, to better understand the unexplored laws of nature and the psychic powers latent in humanity, and to study Eastern traditions such as Hinduism and Buddhism. The founders of the movement, Madame Helena Blavatsky and Colonel Henry Olcott, formally became Buddhists in a public ceremony in Sri Lanka in 1880.

By the beginning of the twentieth century small numbers of Westerners had begun practicing meditation. Some of these went to Asia and engaged seriously with Buddhist religious traditions. At the same time, Asians began bringing their religion to the West. Representatives of Hinduism and Buddhism began teaching in the West in the wake of the World Parliament of Religions held in Chicago in 1893 to promote dialogue among the different religious traditions of the world.

Buddhism and Buddhist cultural influence grew slowly in the West in the first half of the twentieth century; however, Buddhism only became a significant presence in the West in the 1960s. At that time, large numbers of migrants from Buddhist countries began to settle in the West. The practice of Buddhism for them was inseparable from the preservation of their cultural heritage. The Buddhism they established tended to be ethnically based. In the same period, an explosion of interest in Buddhism, and Eastern religion in general, occurred, particularly among young people. This was connected with the counterculture of the 1960s and 70s and the reaction against militarism and the prevailing materialism of Western industrialized economies. Many seekers were looking for a new kind of spiritual conscious-ness and a better way of living in harmony with their fellow beings and the natural environment. To them, Buddhism offered a nonviolent way of living along with a means of realizing a more spiritual consciousness. The practice of meditation was central.

Western interest in Buddhist practice has been principally related to three meditation traditions; the Vipassana (Insight) meditation of the Theravada Buddhist traditions of South-East Asia, Zen Buddhist meditation, and Tibetan Buddhism. These three have, until now, determined the main contours in the development of non-ethnic Western Buddhism.

BEGINNINGS OF WESTERN ZEN

Daisetz T. Suzuki, who went on to become the most influential writer on Zen Buddhism in the world, was sent from Japan to America as a direct consequence of the World Parliament of Religions held in Chicago in 1893. He was sent by his own Zen teacher, Soyen Shaku, to kindle American and European interest in Zen. He succeeded in doing this not only through the many books he wrote, but also by the force of his remarkable personality, which seemed to combine absolute simplicity with all the indefinable qualities of the Far Eastern Taoist or Buddhist sage. Suzuki lived in America continuously from 1897–1908, and then for shorter periods until his death in 1966. He traveled a number of times to Europe, where he was instrumental in promoting interest in Zen.

Suzuki taught for a number of years at Columbia University in New York, where influential writers, poets, composers, artists, psychotherapists and others came to be influenced by him. Suzuki, who belonged to the Rinzai tradition, stressed the sudden breakthrough to enlightenment and koan practice. In his writings and talks, he retold again and again the stories of the unconventional and spontaneous behavior of the old Chinese and Japanese masters. He stressed the spirit of Zen, rather than institutional structures and the ritualized system that had evolved in Japan. He did not dishearten his audience with much discussion of the arduous sitting practice or zazen usually required for the experience of satori.

In 1905, Soyen Shaku sent another of his disciples, Nyogen Senzaki, to America with the instruction that he live there for twenty years before he began teaching. In 1925, Senzaki began quietly teaching Zen meditation to a small number of interested people, including several who were to go on and become recognized Zen masters in their own right. Senzaki, like his own teacher, believed that Zen in Japan had become spiritually impoverished through excessive institutionalization and formalism. He held hopes for an authentic expression of Zen among the foreigners. However, he said that 'Bringing Zen to America is as uncertain as trying to plant a lily by holding it to a rock.'

After World War II, Japan was occupied by the Allied forces. In the post-war period, as a direct result of contact with Zen brought about by the war, a number of Westerners began practicing Zen intensively in Japan. Among these, Walter Nowick went on to become the first Westerner to receive full transmission as a Zen master, and Robert Aitken became a Zen master and a senior teacher to a generation of Western Zen teachers.

ZEN OF THE 'BEAT GENERATION' AND THE COUNTERCULTURE

The 'Beats' were a small group of writers and poets in the 1950s who combined protest against the prevailing norms of contemporary Western society with a search for direct spiritual experience and a new consciousness. The influence of the literary movement that the Beats initiated resulted in a national movement involving many like-minded people that was dubbed the 'beat generation.'

Although they were interested in many forms of spirituality, the main interest of the Beats was Buddhism. The focus was on Zen, which, primarily because of the influence of D. T. Suzuki, was becoming increasingly popular among intellectuals and the avant-garde. Members of the Beats had heard Suzuki's talks at Columbia and read his books. The Beats understood Zen to stress direct spiritual experience, spontaneity, and freedom from the restrictions of dogma, institutional structures and social conventions. Their vision of Zen often promoted the irrational, anti-institutional and iconoclastic aspects of the tradition. Although their understanding is often criticized as one-sided and unbalanced, the Beats were instrumental in promoting Buddhism as a way of personal transformation and in presenting the teachings of Buddhism in the contemporary language of everyday Western life. Foremost among articulators of Zen within the Beats' circle was Alan Watts, whose 'The Way of Zen' (1957) was the most widely read book on the subject in the 1960s.

Stare deep into the world before you as if it were/the void: innumerable holy ghosts, bhuddies/and saviour gods there hide, smiling. All the/atoms emitting light inside wavehood, there is/no personal separation of any of it. A Hummingbird/can come into a house and a hawk will not: so rest/and be assured. While looking for the light, you may suddenly be devoured by the darkness/and find the true light.

Jack Kerouac (*The Scripture of the Golden Eternity*, 1959)

Three important writers of the Beat movement who were interested in Buddhism were:

JACK KEROUAC (1922–69), who inaugurated the 'rucksack revolution' with a vision of life on the road or in the wilderness in his most famous book 'On the Road.' His book 'The Dharma Bums' presented a vision of 'Zen lunatics' leading a spontaneous life of creativity, kindness and spiritual freedom.

ALAN GINSBERG (1926–97), one of the best known and most controversial poets in America, who became deeply interested in Zen in the 1950s. He was intrigued by descriptions of satori and its relation to altered states of consciousness. He eventually committed himself to Tibetan Buddhism.

GARY SNYDER (1930–), a poet and essayist who spent many years during the 1950s and 60s studying Zen formally in Japan and went on to become a Zen teacher and well-known environmental activist.

The Beats were the forerunners of the counterculture and the hippies. The counterculture became a mass movement in the 1960s, fired by the vision of the Beats, the new music (of groups like the Grateful Dead, the Beatles, Jimi Hendrix and Bob Dylan), psychedelic 'mind-expanding' drugs, and radical political thinking. Eastern religion in general was an important ingredient in the mix. Significant numbers of gurus and spiritual teachers began presenting their teachings to receptive audiences. Japanese Zen teachers began establishing centers in the West, bringing with them the forms and rituals of Japanese Zen practice.

The transformation that saw the emergence of Western teachers and forms of Zen that adapted the styles of practice, institutional structures and teacher-student relationship to a Western context began to take shape in the 1960s. An important step in this process was a move from a predominantly intellectual interest and appreciation of Zen to the serious practice of zazen.

CONTEMPORARY WESTERN ZEN

Westerners who had undergone the hard training in Japanese monasteries played an important role in the emergence of Western Zen. They demonstrated that, if Westerners wished to close the gap between intellectual theory and realization, the romance of Zen had to be replaced by the actual experience of concerted Zen practice. Philip Kapleau's *The Three Pillars of Zen* (1965) gave details of Zen training, including lectures for beginners given by Hakuun Yasutani, a Japanese Zen master.

Like D.T. Suzuki, Kapleau and the tradition he followed regarded the dramatic breakthrough to enlightenment to be at the heart of Zen Buddhism. Other teachers put the emphasis elsewhere. They were realizing that the stress on enlightenment needed to be balanced by an understanding of the ordinariness of Zen and of practice as a moment-to-moment realization of the Way. Shunryu Suzuki, a Japanese Soto teacher in San Francisco, established the first Soto Zen monastery in the West based on these principles. A series of his talks was published as *Zen Mind, Beginner's Mind* (1970). This book, widely regarded as a classic of Western Zen, does not mention the words *satori* or *kensho*.

> Zen is not some kind of excitement, but concentration on our usual everyday routine.
>
> Shunryu Suzuki

> If you continue this simple practice every day, you will obtain some wonderful power. Before you attain it, it is something wonderful, but after you attain it, it is nothing special.
>
> Shunryu Suzuki

Western Zen, along with Western Buddhism in general, differs significantly from its Asian counterparts. Some of the most important differences are:

• an emphasis on lay practice. The ordained monks (and to a much lesser extent, nuns) have been central to Asian Buddhist practice. Western Buddhism, especially Zen, is predominantly a lay movement. The Buddhist community (sangha) is not thought of only in terms of those who have taken monastic ordination. Both practitioners and Zen teachers are, for the most part, lay people. Monastic ordination does not enhance the prestige of a teacher or of practitioners.

• an increased role for women as practitioners and teachers. Buddhist practice in Asia has been largely a male preserve. Very few women teachers have risen to positions of prominence. In Western Buddhism, women make up more than half the practitioners, and significant numbers of women are recognized teachers, including several Zen masters.

• a greater concern for social change and justice. Buddhism is not only seen in terms of withdrawal and introspection. It also may involve active engagement in social and political issues. For many, the wisdom aspect of Buddhism must be balanced by the active practice of compassion, both on the immediate personal level and more widely in the social and political spheres. Prominent leaders of Asian Buddhism such as the Tibetan Dalai Lama and the Vietnamese Zen master Thich Nhat Hanh have also advocated balancing meditative withdrawal with active engagement in the world. Significantly, the Dalai Lama and Aung San Suu Kyi, the Burmese opposition leader, have both been awarded the Nobel Peace Prize. Thich Nhat Hanh was also nominated for the Prize by the American Civil Rights leader Martin Luther King. Thich Nhat Hanh coined the expression 'engaged Buddhism,' and has interpreted its significance to Western activists and meditators.

ISSUES IN WESTERN ZEN

The 1960s and and early 1970s saw the rapid growth of Western Zen as centers were established, books were published, and an upsurge in enthusiasm for Zen was evidenced. A series of charismatic Asian Zen teachers seemingly provided certainty in the tradition and an authoritative voice in decision-making and on matters of doctrine and practice. However, by the beginning of the 1980s, Western Zen was entering troubled waters.

A defining issue was the role and authority of the teacher. Confusion arose when the behavior of some teachers was found wanting. The main areas of contention related to sexual misconduct and drinking. The charges made against these teachers raised questions about their spiritual credentials. More generally, these situations questioned the institution of dharma transmission, which saw the title of 'roshi' (master) handed on from teacher to disciple. The failures and limitations of some teachers, both Asian and Western, also raised questions about the place of kensho in the Zen path. The experience of kensho and a long training through the koan system did not seem to guarantee against human fallibility in a number of areas.

The Western Zen that is still emerging has moved away from the hierarchical model of authority typical of Asian Buddhism to more egalitarian styles in keeping with modern Western values. This has gone hand in hand with an acceptance of the teacher as human and fallible, and a recognition that authority in one area, for example spiritual practice, does not necessarily entail authority in other areas, for example, administrative or financial. It has also involved clarifying what constitutes an appropriate teacher-student relationship that does not abuse the role of teacher or student in an exploitative way. Dharma transmission as the defining act in setting spiritual authority has been de-emphasized, and is now seen to have a role in conjunction with other tests including critical scrutiny of a teacher's behavior. Many Western Zen teachers are now cautious about over-reliance on koan practice. The intense experiences that can arise from koan practice, by themselves, do not make a person enlightened. The experiences must be integrated into the whole person and actualized in the practitioner's life. This involves a process of maturation. In the 'pressure-cooker' approach of some styles of intense practice in which the student is pushed towards the breakthrough of kensho, important stages in the maturation of the student can be bypassed. This can result in a person (even a teacher) appearing to be more spiritually advanced than he or she actually is. Many teachers today are careful to balance the intense experience of breakthrough with moment-to-moment development of awareness. Some Zen teachers are integrating awareness training from other Buddhist traditions, such as Vipassana (Insight) meditation from the Theravada tradition. A few teachers advocate the use of techniques from Western psychotherapy in conjunction with zazen.

Less contentious, but nonetheless important, have been issues of ritual and other cultural forms. To what extent should Japanese and Korean styles, language of chanting, rituals, protocol, dress, architecture, diet and so on be retained in Western Zen practice? There has been a spectrum of responses to this question. In general, teachers are adopting English chanting (sometimes combined with other languages), Western modes of dress and so on.

Distilling the Essence

APPRECIATING OUR LIVES AND THE PRESENT MOMENT

> This present birth and death is the life of the Buddha. If you reject it
> with distaste, you lose the life of the Buddha.
>
> Dogen Zenji

One of the things Dogen Zenji meant by this was not to expect to find enlightenment apart from the here and now. He says we should not reject the life we have in favor of some imagined better alternative. If we do, we risk missing all the joys and possibilities of our present life. Nor do we need to abandon the world to undertake spiritual practice. Going to some other country, to a cave, or to a monastery is not essential. Nor, according to Zen teachers, should we imagine the peace of nirvana is to be realized somewhere else other than in the midst of the world, in the midst of change, and in the midst of difficulty. This understanding is essential to Zen Buddhism. In one sense, there is nothing at all to be done, nowhere else to go, no other life to lead other than the one we have. As Lin-chi, the founder of the Lin-chi (Rinzai) School, says:

> Just be ordinary and nothing special. Relieve your bowels, pass
> water, put on your clothes and eat your food. When you are tired go
> and lie down. Ignorant people may laugh at me but the wise will
> understand.

The difficulty is that we are not willing or able to fully accept and appreciate our own lives. Usually we are so busy and distracted that we are not fully aware of what we are doing or of who we are. When we are not busy, we seek something to take us away from the present moment and from ourselves. We always want something more or something else. According to Zen, most of us have, in large measure, lost touch with ourselves, with our own lives, and with those around us. But Zen teaches that the true joy in our lives does not lie somewhere else or in being someone different. It can only be found in the present moment and in ourselves. Zen offers us methods to overcome our distractions and to become aware of the here and now. It also offers us methods to come to know ourselves and our Buddha nature – to discover that we are not the impoverished beings that we might have imagined ourselves to be.

PRACTICAL STEPS WE CAN TAKE

• Try to simplify our lives. This will facilitate clarity and give us the opportunity to slow down and to appreciate ourselves and others, especially those we are close to and love. It helps if we can identify what is really important to us and then concentrate on those things. One technique that can help us clarify this is to imagine what our priorities would be if we knew we had only a short time left to live.

• Limit our desires. Our hunger for possessions and emotional (and even spiritual) experiences arises because we feel something is lacking in ourselves. As we pay more attention to the present moment, we begin to realize that we do not need a lot of things to be happy. As the Vietnamese master Thich Nhat Hahn says, 'We can be very happy just by being aware of what is in front of us.'

• Find a suitable practice and set aside a regular time to do it. Meditation on the breath is an ideal way of bringing us back to the present moment and to ourselves. We can count the breaths, follow the breath, or use a verse to integrate breathing and awareness of the present moment. Alternatively, we can simply sit with awareness in the present moment without using any special technique, or meditate using a koan. Even setting aside ten minutes a day will make a difference.

• Be aware of our motivation for our spiritual practice and for our daily activities. If our motivation is selfish, we are unlikely to find satisfaction in our activities or in our spiritual practice. When we awaken in the morning, we can think briefly how we are going to use the day so that it might be beneficial both to ourselves and to others. When we begin meditation, we can check our motivation and express the wish that both ourselves and others be happy.

• We can use moments during the day to bring our attention back to the present moment, to relax, to be aware of our breath, of our body, of our thoughts and emotions, and to appreciate what is happening in the world around us. One way to do this is to use verses to help us tune in to the present moment. Even just a few verses can be a powerful aid to awareness. We can compose suitable verses ourselves or use verses from Buddhist tradition.

> The mind can go in a thousand directions.
> But on this path, I walk in peace.

Further Reading

Aitken, Robert, *Taking the Path of Zen*, North Point Press, San Francisco, 1982.

Beck, Joko, *Everyday Zen: Love and Work*, Harper & Row, New York, 1989.

Gethin, Rupert, *The Foundations of Buddhism*, Oxford University Press, Oxford, 1998.

Glassman, Bernard & Fields, Rick, *Instructions to the Cook: A Zen Master's Lessons in Living a Life that Matters*, Bell Tower, New York, 1996.

Herrigel, E., *Zen in the Art of Archery*, Vintage, New York, 1971.

Kapleau, Philip, *The Three Pillars of Zen*, Harper & Row, New York, 1969.

Lowenstein, Tom, *The Vision of the Buddha*, Macmillan/Duncan Baird, London, 1996.

Nhat Hanh, Thich, *Present Moment, Wonderful Moment: Mindfulness Verses for Daily Living*, Parallax Press, Berkeley, 1990.

Nhat Hanh, Thich, *Peace is Every Step: The Path of Mindfulness in Everyday Life*, Bantam, New York, 1992.

Suzuki, D.T. , *Introduction to Zen Buddhism*, Causeway Books, New York, 1974.

Suzuki, Shunryu, *Zen Mind, Beginner's Mind*, Weatherhill, New York & Tokyo, 1970.

Watts, Alan, *The Way of Zen*, Vintage, New York, 1989.

Glossary and Names

Amida - Japanese *Amitabha*

Amitabha - Buddha of boundless light; Buddha of the Western Paradise or Pure Land

Amitofo - Chinese *Amitabha*

anatman - non-self

Ashoka - emperor of India in third century BC

Avalokiteshvara - bodhisattva of compassion

Basho - most famous exponent of Japanese haiku poetry

Bodhidharma - Indian monk who brought Zen Buddhism to China

bodhisattva - literally 'enlightenment being.' A being close to becoming a buddha who works for the benefit of others

Buddha - enlightened one or awakened one

Chan - Chinese Zen

Cha-no-yu - Japanese tea ceremony

Chao-chu - renowned Chinese master of the Tang dynasty, famous for the koan 'mu'

Chinul - most important figure in Korean Zen (Son) Buddhism

Confucianism - moral and religious system based on the teachings of Confucius (551-479 BC)

dai kensho - complete enlightenment

dharma - teachings of the Buddha

dhyana - meditative absorption or deep concentration

do - Way, Japanese equivalent of Tao

Dogen Zenji - founder of the Soto school in Japan

dokusan - private meeting with Zen teacher

duhkha - suffering or unsatisfactoriness

emptiness - absence of independent existence (Sanskrit *shunyata*)

Esai - founder of Japanese Rinzai school

haiku - Japanese poetic form

Hakuin - reformer of Japanese Rinzai school

hara - energy center in the abdomen, just below the navel

Hatha yoga - Indian system of psycho-physical discipline involving postures, breathing and meditation

Hinduism - the predominant religion of India

Hui-neng - Sixth patriarch of Chinese Zen Buddhism

Joshu - Japanese *Chao-chu*

karma - the moral law of cause and effect

kensho - literally seeing into one's own nature; breakthrough to enlightenment

kinhin - walking meditation

koan - short and often enigmatic saying of a Zen master, set as an object of meditation

Kuan Yin - female form of Avalokiteshvara (bodhisattva of compassion) in Chinese Buddhism

kung-an - (Chinese) koan

Lao-tzu - founder of Taoism

Lin-chi - founder of Lin-chi (Japanese Rinzai) School of Chinese Zen

Lin-chi School - Zen school founded by Lin-chi

Mahakashyapa - senior disciple of Shakyamuni Buddha

Mahayana - the Great Way; a form of Buddhism that emphasizes the bodhisattva ideal

Maitreya - the future Buddha

Manjushri – bodhisattva of wisdom

mantra – sacred sound used in meditation

mondo – Zen dialogue between a master and a student

mu – literally 'No!'; the most widely used koan

Mumonkan – thirteenth century collection of koans

Nine Mountains Schools – name of Korean Zen schools

nirvana – end of suffering; Buddhist enlightenment

Obaku School – one school of Japanese Zen Buddhism

parinirvana – the final entry into nirvana on the dissolution of the body

patriarch – a principal lineage holder in early Zen tradition

Prajna Paramitra Sutras – the 'Perfection of Wisdom Scriptures'

Rinzai – Japanese *Lin-chi*

Rinzai School – Japanese *Lin-chi* school

roshi – Zen master

samadhi – meditation, especially concentration

samsara – cycle of birth and death

samurai – a member of the Japanese warrior class

sangha – Buddhist community

satori – Japanese term for the experience of enlightenment or awakening

Sen-no-Rikyu – most famous exponent of the tea ceremony

sesshin – Zen meditation practice retreat

Shakyamuni Buddha – the historical Buddha

Shen-hsiu – disciple of the Sixth patriach

shikantaza – 'just sitting'

shunyata – emptiness; absence of independent existence

Siddhartha Gautama – name of the historical Buddha

skandhas - physical and mental factors that make up the person

Son - Korean Zen

Soto School - Japanese *Tsao-tung* school

Sumi-e - Japanese painting and calligraphy

sutras - Buddhist scriptures

Tao - the Way

Tao Te Ching - principal text of Taoism, composed by Lao-tzu

Taoism - Chinese philosophical and religious system established by Lao-tzu

teisho - dharma talk given by a Zen master

Tetsugan - scholar monk of the Obaku School

The Four Noble Truths - the fundamental teachings of Shakyamuni Buddha

The Noble Eightfold Path - the path leading to the end of suffering

The Three Jewels - Buddha, Dharma and Sangha

The Three Principal Aspects of the Path - conduct, meditation and wisdom

Theravada - 'the doctrine of the elders'; the predominant form of Buddhism in South East Asia

Theravada - principal form of Buddhism in South-East Asia

Thien - Vietnamese Zen

Tsao-tung School - Chinese school of Zen Buddhism (Japanese *Soto*)

Vipassana - insight meditation practiced in Theravada Buddhism

wen-ta - (Chinese) mondo

Western Paradise - the paradise of the Buddha Amitabha

wu-wei - non-action or non-doing

zafu - meditation cushion

zazen - sitting meditation

zendo - large meditation room

Published by Lansdowne Publishing Pty Ltd
Sydney NSW 2001, Australia

© Copyright 2001 Lansdowne Publishing Pty Ltd

Commissioned by Deborah Nixon
Production Manager: Sally Stokes
Text: Peter Oldmeadow
Illustrator: Sue Ninham
Designer: Sue Rawkins
Editor: Patricia Dacey
Project Co-ordinator: Kate Merrifield

National Library of Australia Cataloguing-in-Publication Data
Oldmeadow, Peter.
Zen.
ISBN 1 86302 746 7.
1. Zen Buddhism - Philosophy. 2. Zen Buddhism - HIstory.
3. Zen Buddhism - Rituals. I. Title.
294.3927

The quotations on page 66 are from *Zen Mind, Beginner's Mind* (1970) by Shunryu Suzuki,
and are reproduced by kind permission of Weatherhill Publishers, USA. The quotation on
page 64 is from *The Scripture of Golden Eternity*, City Lights Books, San Francisco, 1994.
Full effort has been made to obtain permissions for quotations within this book. Any
omissions or corrections will be rectified in future editions.

Set in Interstate on QuarkXPress
Printed in Singapore by Tien Wah Press (Pte) Ltd